Northbound

poems by

Avery Lane

Finishing Line Press
Georgetown, Kentucky

Northbound

Copyright © 2023 by Avery Lane
ISBN 979-8-88838-276-9 First Edition
All rights reserved under International and Pan-American Copyright Conventions. No part of this book may be reproduced in any manner whatsoever without written permission from the publisher, except in the case of brief quotations embodied in critical articles and reviews.

ACKNOWLEDGMENTS

Thank you to my family, who have enthusiastically supported my most meaningful journeys, and without whom this book would not be possible. Thank you to my friend Aura- for the poetry we wrote when we were supposed to be scientists, and for traveling with me down very difficult roads.

Publisher: Leah Huete de Maines
Editor: Christen Kincaid
Cover Art: Aura Raulo
Author Photo: David Wang
Cover Design: Elizabeth Maines McCleavy

Order online: www.finishinglinepress.com
also available on amazon.com

Author inquiries and mail orders:
Finishing Line Press
PO Box 1626
Georgetown, Kentucky 40324
USA

Table of Contents

The Beginning and the End ... 1
Place of Thunder ... 3
The World Builder ... 4
Blood in Sock ... 5
Practicalities ... 6
Excavation ... 7
On Doves ... 8
The desert is a tough old broad ... 9
Phenology ... 10
Sea Plane ... 11
Basin Post-fire ... 12
Kearny, AZ ... 14
Lesson of Snakes ... 16
Time Travel ... 17
Yellow Flowers ... 18
Unexpecting ... 19
Leaving Strawberry ... 20
No Longer Theirs ... 21
The Spider's Decision ... 22
Leaving Flagstaff ... 23
Ni' ... 25
Horses and Salamanders ... 26
What I see, what I feel, what is happening ... 27
Side Canyon ... 28
Haiku for Utah Agave ... 29
Haiku for Canyon Wall ... 30
Aging on the ridgeline ... 31
Mammal ... 32
Scarring of Aspen ... 33
The Collage Artist ... 34
The Walking Rock ... 35

The Beginning and the End

Past the makeshift sign, reading: *don't
go on, for your own safety,* the webs
of neon orange no longer taut between
barbed wire; rising above the native
grasses, spreading their roots in furious
ignorance, over the boundary;

the Wall bisects the bloated, fading
sky. Severe, medieval, a swarm
of symbolism, protecting no one.
All metal, choked up with drying blood.

Beside the stone-grey obelisk,
marking the beginning, or the end,
a dirt road stretches surgically
and eternally, east, across
the belly of the grassland. The threat
of snow stroking our backs, we drive

north, the Wall a cruel stitch of our
periphery, and dad tells me how
they use infrared imaging
technology to detect those

crossing the border. It is another
set of eyes which doesn't need the sky
to see, capturing just enough humanity,
deciding who and what to discard. A deer
could be mistaken for a person, perhaps
one with a fever; tongue a swollen,

sleeping moth. A person could be
mistaken for a deer. To tell the
difference, the overseers have to pay
attention to the way those warm

animal bodies move across the land.
Do they walk as if following the
distribution of grasses, or do they seem tied
to a northern star? Are they spaced out, as a herd
would forage? Do they graze or do they walk

a silent line, motion undeterred as distant
symphonies of rabbit scream drown
in celebratory howl? Do they walk
on hands or hooves? What is their temperature,
how does one measure the heat of a small

body held to the center of another? How
does one quantify terror, in a forager,
or in a wanderer? Must they walk on all fours,
like prey? What does a body look like,
with or without understanding, with or
without allegiance, to the Walls human beings build?

Place of Thunder

The path flanks the meandering
spine of mountains, who slowly remove
my faces and turn them into clouds

drifting further, and further north.
I think that by the end, I may no longer
have a face at all, mirrors overgrown

by moss and the wind will keep me
cocooned in this dream. Canyons fall
soft beside the trail's barely edges, exhaling

breaths of blue and grey, the fleeing
indignant flocks of jays, emerge busy
from the scrub-smeared hillsides.

The trees grow wilder with elevation,
their branches beseeching god, wringing
their coil against the skies. Other branches

sag, clung to their undersides are bits of chalk-
like snow, the fragile teeth of trees
loosening around a dozing gum.

Their distant brethren sleep facing north, float
as in a dream, the mountain seethes with gauzy
mauvish foam; the sum of their skeletons. I expect

them to awaken, and set the mountain alight
with green and wing. Spring waits in my bones
like a face fading from memory.

The World Builder

Each poem is a world built.
When we leave these anxious

little planets, we leave rearranged, less
explained. Each poem is a sweet

little curse; and we are grateful, even as they burn
us. We kiss our hands, eyes closed, and recall

how the kingdom rose; bloomed from soil
thought useless. How the raw material

of seas preserved the sky's great bolt,
long enough to translate our burning

into the stuff of tongues. We return and walk
around in poems, but we will never see them

as they once were. We will never be
who we were, when we built them.

Blood in Sock

I am seeing new dimensions. I am not afraid.
The wind removes my pain, which had become

overgrown, a thicket of tangled words.
My pain now bleeds into my sock! I shout

at the tawny oceans of grass. *I can see it.
I can heal it.* Mountains are far behind me now,

mountains of yesterday. Now the breath
is everything. No matter what else is happening,

I return, to the only escape from absurdity
I'm now aware of, the last thing we do

before dying. I bite the air and unify
with the landscape, the beauty underlying

solitude's wrathful wing, and I bleed,
and I breathe, and I sing.

Practicalities

A slow burning angel dies
on my tongue, as I wind
up from rock and cow
to alligator juniper.
This creek is perfect- clear and
cold- over the sleeping red leaves,
large as my palms, and the blue swallows
every cloud, very slowly,
as I pause practicalities, for the
hawk who watched me, to fly,
silently, over the canyon she loves.

Excavation

The sun and moon
hang in the same sky.
They share a pink cloud
destined for fracture.

How I've loved.
Painfully, and wildly;
enough for a lifetime.
Wind and walking

set loose one thousand
little dams in me, flooding
the foothills with gloom.
I will melt and splinter,

under the sun. Heart split open
and plundered, by the golden
scar of morning. Until I am as
clean and unburdened as bone.

On Doves

Cottonwoods line the meekly
flowing washes, the tang of pollen
filling our noses. The *Populus*
of my childhood stand trembling,
psychedelic green.

Mesquite bosques deflect
the sun's steady pour, until
the earth begins to slowly revolve
itself away, leaving that watery
orb weeping light into the hinge of the land.

Sitting on a stone wall, swelling
feet prone to the breeze, I listen
to the white-winged doves.
Just a dove, so says the avid avian
observer, not knowing each

of these birds are made by hand,
molded into being from silver clay
tinged with azure. Some delicate
thumb presses a solid black line
into the cheek like time

grows in rock. Some wayward bits of blue
sky settle around the way doves see
the world. Their startling is the sound
of the dappled light of morning. In a web
of their calling, I am visited

by a new texture of longing, some rare
species of hope. The feeling is
a friendship which cannot last long,
merely due to circumstance; one which
begins and ends on a single train ride,

far from home. I am reminded of earlier
days, before words began and ended
everything we knew. What we thought was
possible unhinged our minds, as we molded
ourselves from clay, and sky settled on our eyes.

The desert is a tough old broad

You can keep your ferns,
your storied undergrowth,
your arrogant orchid.

You can keep your blackberries,
and maple leaves, sleeping softly
on the cold floor of creeks.

Keep the humus, so soft you can put
a fist through it, and fragrant as a book
of spells. Boil your nettle leaves,

keep your coddled lianas, your
prima donna, mountain-loving
lichen. I'll stay home, tottering

on the edge of dehydration,
I will eat lunch next to the remains
of something's face, in the only patch of

shade for miles. Ocotillos bloom, grounded
in limestone, vermillion mouths
biting a sky always wide open

like a life in crisis. I am laughing
at the heat, the sun's touch like being
in love with someone you don't like

very much. Lizards and rabbits flee,
humble from aridity, fast hearts beat
the vivid into cholla, a ruinous purple,

and the saguaros, our grandmothers,
and grandfathers, tell me stories as I pass,
arms raised, holding me up.

Phenology

Something intangible passes through
us, too ephemeral to name.

Look to the phenology, unfolding
the days, how some flowers bloom

as others wane, lending each other
color in accordance with the drunken

stupor of beetles and bees.
Where just a day ago, the fairy dusters

screamed a brilliant pink, now fade
to bird-down with every passing mile,

replaced by thistles in all their forms,
from puckered mouths magenta to full

bursts of bleeding violet. Sleepy yellow
flowers under storm clouds grow in trampled

dirt, as if they thrive on the meandering
of hooves, and begin to undulate their petals

from brain-like folds into eyes blinking
about our ankles. Halos of beckoning

poppy around bundles of stamen become
an orange so orange the afterimage haunts

us, the blue sky full of poppies, our palms full
of bloom. Flowers today and tomorrow- not.

We know joy passes as a busy guest amongst the
blank yawn of our bones, but gratefully,

this is reflected, concretely and predictably,
in something as real as flowers.

Sea Plane

I met a pilot
at the top of a hill.
He didn't know where
he was going, and I had the strange
peace of someone who has much
further to walk.

He liked to disappear in the
clouds. He flew to Lake
Roosevelt last weekend, and slept
beside the plane, covered in
dew, while the passengers got
drunk in the harbor.

His grandmother is 94
and was a pilot also.
They had reached an understanding:
they would wait for her
to die, so he could move to Alaska and
fly sea planes.

Every morning, he sat her up
in bed, and said *You're not dead yet!*
He wanted to disappear in the clouds,
he got that from her. They laughed
over oatmeal and coffee. They could hardly
wait for her to die.

Basin Post-fire

Time rolls like an egg
from a nest. Shatters before

my feet, and the yolk
spreads over the land until

I believe it is under
the ocean again.

From the ridgeline,
the manzanita are a silent

forest of kelp, all in
different stages of fruiting

and leaf drop. Bleeding
bark, burnt bark,

bark that's given up.
Remains of yucca sprawl

inside circles of ash. The soil
is white and fingers

of the wind have drawn
healing hexes between

the charred bodies
of trees. I am on land

healing itself, I am inside
a ghost resurrecting.

I am catching a doll
blinking, I can feel

the land remembering
cold currents over

its canyons and sea shells
working up out of the dirt

of its summits, and memories
of salt and darkness.

Kearny, AZ

Established in 1958,
back when mining towns were
segregated, separate streams
of overworked men rushed hungry
to the same copper vein.

A man compliments dad's
truck, as it's the kind of town
where this speaks volumes about
a person's character. A good truck
could compensate for nearly

anything. *A nearby town caught fire,*
a woman explains to the pizza
place owner, *but dad and grandad's place
is ok.* I imagine a white-paneled house
closing its eyes in the smoke.

The pizza is covered in gratuitous
piles of black olive, still glistening
from the brine of their jars. Everything
is served on stiff paper, like we all
might have to leave at any moment.

Cottonwoods surround the Gila,
their canopy some sort of inverted
green sky. I want to fall into it,
and wake up on the other side.
We sleep beside a tributary

just south of town, with a train
track running through it.
Somewhere downstream, teenagers
drink beer and play music from the speakers
of a matte-black pick-up.

It feels far too much like America,
all brown water and a blank face
carved into distant mountains,
for which there are three separate
names. The river is a tea of mine

tailings, my mouth is full of theory.
I'm choking, and I'm
knowing, we are all leading
different lives, and seeing
different things.

Lesson of Snakes

We had lost our fleeing
and our flinching. Before shadow

and thunder, our skin no longer
rose, eyes no longer expanded

to swallow whole the details. We had seen
everything, been hurt by it all.

Our heads were a constant storm
of static, waves trapped inside

a glass box. We were day-old moths,
sensory velvet of our wings fading

in life's negligent palms. One day,
we narrowly avoided a snake, and oh,

how it rattled euphoria into our heart
and lung! We remembered the jolt

of being animal, and every member in
our long bloodline sang out the same

life-affirming rhyme! The snake's
warning, the pre-strike choreography

imprinted somewhere deep,
showed us we still recognize danger.

The snake left our hearts
beating, bodies intact and

shaking with death-defying
joy. We bolt, and we want to live.

Time Travel

My hands no longer seem to be my own.
In and out of focus, the hands of others'
alternately grow and dim, layers of
skin having seen different suns, and a
differing number of years.

My ancestors time travel
through my hands. Knuckles
swell and collapse, salt and
softness carve my fluctuating
life line. My nails wax and wane

as moons, crescents blacken
with the soil of millennia,
shorten and lengthen; fickle,
full of time. My hands are taut
with cold, warp with grime and

water, peel in relentless
sun; my hands grow numb.
Every she is in my hands,
warming on the rocks, working
the soil, loitering in the grass.

Yellow Flowers
    (for dad)

On an April morning, one can
sit and think on what the bees know.

A diversity of sparrows call from canyon
to canyon. A snake crosses the path, lifting its head

at our steps. The cottonwoods form a bright green
seam along the vein of the land, an inverted sky

of trembling leaves. And yellow flowers grow
past our knees, clinging to the creek bed.

Yellow flowers, and fathers, we know
Lay the roots for the water's path. A tendril

maze guides all the babbling of the stream child,
and as sure as the bees dunk their velvet heads into

the golden eyes of stamen, we know that yellow flowers
and fathers keep the water and light from dissolving

into rootless sand, so that we may sit beside the creek bed
on an April morning, and think on what the bees know.

Unexpecting

Just when you knew for sure that
sadness had the notion
to settle on you, unexpectedly;
that only doom could slip inside
your landscape, without apology,
without reason; you will walk

through a field of yellow, dying
grass. and though the sun still seethes
of late afternoon, and no matter which
way you hold your head or brim
your hat, the burning stays on your
cheek; though the wilting brick-red ants

have just begun to find their way home,
though you have left a jade river behind,
and great expanses await; the field of yellow,
dying grass will begin to bloom with the song
of crickets, and an unreasonable joy will break
open inside of you: that bright clamp about the

walls of the heart which sends its beating into
the chaos of the present. and you may ask,
why here? why this place? about the dry
ridgeline, dusty cattle tracks roaming
between the humble junipers, whose bark withers
in the sun of the day's final call? just when you

consider yourself empty, all spring's green left
behind you and your hands swollen with time,
you will find a clear pool of water, in a canyon
no one ever named, look into it, and wash
your face with the trembling
sky you find there.

Leaving Strawberry

Walking away from Town.
Every breath, every step, brings me
further into unity with the world.

The highway, etched into the
land by some great bored
machine, recedes, as does the sound,

and the sense, to the absurd metal boxes
hurrying along the static tongue of heat-
strewn tar. Thoughts become as brittle

and bound for decomposition, as the
oaks' late spring leaves. The path, for the
first mile worn to dust by city shoe, grows faint.

Needle underfoot now, the pines call
me in. My head fades to wind, within
a sun-smeared copse of trees.

My face too, forms a pool of water,
drying and filling like a seasonal spring.
Unreliable: at times a trickle; other times,

a pond, wreathed in billows of green.
Cardinals become my body; I am all wing
and beak. I am the flitting wound

against the cone-laced face
of the hills, climbing northward onto
the rim of this land.

No Longer Theirs

In a motel room in Strawberry,
Arizona, the mirror slowly loses
its gauze of steam, and I unmake all
the words we've used to talk about bodies
in the past. All I see are smears
of peach and cloud, tall trees and
ways of joining the world, softness
and peeled bark run ragged with sap,
ants like pencil dashes leaving the powdery
mouths of their homes. My body is no
longer mine, or yours, or theirs.
A land without sovereignty, at last.
You cannot fence it in.
There is no binary that can describe the body's
abandonment of its extra parts; its burning
skin; pain planted like a seed among its rigging;
toenails ejected, vestiges of the claws
of all our tree-bound days.

The Spider's Decision

She moves along the forest floor,
or maybe floats from branch to

branch as a deliberate wayward
fairy – what is the breadth of her sky?

Surely not this whole gray mess,
into which peach and mauve are

softly spooned, vibrant behind the bodies
of the pines? Did she consider the angles

of light, whispered from Great Nowhere,
the Great Everywhere, as she stole between those

hardy little mountain flowers of joy-drunk
yellow, and luciferian pink?

Did the flowers guide her thin
legs and soft body, clumsy as embroidery

cleanly ripped from linen fields, sparsely
sprinkled as they are amongst the snow-

chilled ground, as though a spell had fallen
piecewise from a pocket?

She must have arrived at this felled
log, and considered the span of her own

life, how it would not outlast the wood's
calm decomposition, its gentle joining

with the longing soil, as lovers do decay
into a single material ache. She chose this

open black eye, walked the soil's lip
into a tunnel round as the whole world,
and hung her shroud of shimmering web.

Leaving Flagstaff

I am beneath a tree on the snow-
flattened grasses, long since dried
under the lithe body of afternoon.

I have walked through
groves of leafless aspen, into
which were etched forgotten names

and dates which meant a whole lot to
someone, at some time. There is a sort
of desperate simplicity in our longing for

preservation, carving I am here all we
can do, knifing a misunderstanding of
carbon into the pale faces of trees.

On the way here, a restored pond learns
how to live in this prairie once again.
A couple stands at its edge, coaxing two

identical black dogs to swim in manic circles,
their earnestness approaching a happy line
between endearing and grotesque. The dogs

bark viciously at my pack as I filter brown
water into plastic. The ritual quiets the mad bark
of brain and hound alike. Here now, a pair of

robins talk each other into sunset, a brilliant
orange burning between quills of west-facing
pine. Their calls are complements, folding into

each other as wings fit onto bodies,
so seamlessly I do not notice when they stop.
I have left another city behind, a motel room doused

in cleaning supply, and the inexplicable nightstand
bible, all starch and indigo in its clean drawer where
time has stopped proceeding. A small bathroom

window, bordered by studious lines of ants, where one can
exchange the sting of false clean for the queasy
breath of route 66. Screens and plates and follow

up questions, away; I float up and up and
up, out of transaction, away from logical,
angular avenue. I lay beneath deep blue

and star, the robins all gone silent,
orange leached from the western sky by
the earth's revolving melancholy.

Ni'

There are days when I cannot separate howling
wind from mind. I've come too far now, to see

the mountains once summited, and even
tucked within a brief respite of ocher-laden

juniper, I summon the perseverance of flies.
They swarm as though wanting something beyond

my body, deep within me, seeking some rotting
thought. Why must the journey's end curdle so

suddenly? Why does it hasten what has been so long
kept at bay: the cold knot of *now what?* If I could stay

in these eternal walking days, lacking name and
narrative, perhaps this wind could cease its battering

on the rigging of my nerves. In the Apache language,
the root of the words for *land* and *mind* are the same.

As my mind returns to its comfortable pain, those old
divvy wormed haunts, and hypotheticals

descend, terrible and winged on the architecture
of Self, cruel in their detail, I think *has the land done*

this to me, made of me a sieve losing all the world's
awe? An endless parched scrubland of birdlack

and juniper, a strange grass grows not tall but in desperate
fungal clump of the dullest sage, as though its hue stolen

by the predatory lavender beast of sky above.
Or instead, *does my mind create this landscape?*

For the small strip of gold and blue between the storm
clouds and the line where our vision flails, makes things up-

may be just as thin as my own fragments of hope,
swimming in my face.

Horses and Salamanders

A wildlife pond draws golden
eagle, coyote, and girl. We share
in what we need. An old man arrives and
tells me about the wild horses, escaped

from the res', a mess of feral and tame,
you can only tell by the eye. He talks
about them with a tenderness rare
in American men, like they were the part

of his family who went their own way, who
no one ever hears from, anymore; but he can
remember at least one summer, slipping away
until the memory is a copy of a copy of a

copy of itself. The pond is full of water dogs,
he explains, *you know, water dogs!* we volley
descriptors until we find a common word. Horses
emerge from the forest just then. The old man

points a gnarled finger to *a foal,* tucks his pliers
deeper into a denim pocket. *So we know
at least that one is wild, felt neither rope
nor hand.* Sam the dog rests his muzzle

politely between paws. Sometimes, the salamanders
don't leave the water in time. they grow and
grow and grow, unrecognizable. Sometimes, he finds
the horses' bodies in hidden forest trenches.

*They had been running between the trees,
and didn't see, and fell right in.
If they do not leave the water in time, it is too late.
They never become salamanders.*

What I see, what I feel, what is happening (for Aura)

Cottonwoods frame the creek bed. A trembling
green against the worn face of the inner gorge, rust
royal, a haze of sun softening the eons.
A vermillion bird, eye and wing soaked in black,
clings to the thinnest branches, when an unexpected
wind from nowhere arrives. Absurd primates, mortal

clueless burning beings. We sit in creeks and revel
in our insignificance, not knowing love's definition,
feeling it always. As children grown in the nest
of mountains, the distances ever call us. I don't want
to do anything, except lie in the grass and burn.
Make me a substrate, from which dove-grey spiders leap

across the light. We point to birds and murmur things
the other doesn't hear, but understands anyway.
My brother pulls a pair of sunglasses out of the water,
a tangle of algae where a face should be. I make my mind
the creek. Some thoughts flourish between buoyant
blankets of moss, freckle the rocks green and gold
and red. Others are bound for downstream, into the great
teal river, the grateful vein of god.

Side Canyon

the creek
once full of angels
becomes a
humble brown stream

I am full
of a kind of
hope I don't remember
losing

my eyes burn
with joy at the smallest
beings and breezes
at one with whatever

ground I stand on
whatever sky holds my head
in its hands
I do not feel Alone

do you exist in a
side canyon, cocooned
against the carnival
of identity

Haiku for Utah Agave

The yellow staircase,
burning with carpenter bees,
makes the bluest sky.

Haiku for Canyon Wall

Our tongues stole the crown.
Stone mother, weeping eons.
World's womb and bone.

Aging on the ridgeline

Though in our youth we found pleasure
in the pressure of fertilizer on our
wandering tongues, time places us
on lichen-mottled overhangs looking east.
Breathing in the restorative air of mixed conifer,
that grey-green fur of the north, woodpeckers
call so loud they set the air to blur, dimming
even the wide-eyed sight of the aspens' bark.
We know a deepening has begun,
from somewhere it had long lain a cherished
safe-kept seed, and our heart, though it's shed
the topsoil's thrill and wayward meter of hurried love,
has morphed into dark humus, unbeknownst
to those who had felt its beat against their own.
Centuries of trampling, and regenerative fire,
and the layered wilting of bodies, have made
a bed of our hearts, reaping forests anew,
with foundations which seemed to take all of time itself.

Mammal

My body, now, is of a different sort and skew.
My face is a conveyor of symbol, it stretches and

wrinkles, opens and closes, to send messages
across the great chasm, that yawn between Self

and Other, rendered and wrecked and ensnared
by the filters between us. My muscles and joints

carry me across unimaginable distances,
in a loyalty my mind could never hope to achieve;

my feet become sacred. My skin and hair keep
me warm. Sweat, no longer a nuisance, is the barometer

of my effort, tells me when to slow down, and when
to keep going. I burrow in the quiet places trees

encircle, my eyes find the flat on any forest floor,
where I can sleep, sheltered from wind,
unadorned by dew, a mammal under the stars.

Scarring of Aspen

With each new branch, a wound
blooms in the pale face of aspen

trees. Bark-born eyes open
as the trees, in their new height,

discard their skirts of sun-keen
arms. From a fire-ravaged slope

they thrived, not in spite of, but
owing to acidic loam and the great

gap in canopy. By some grace,
the saplings were missed by roaming

hooves and teeth. Tall now,
a single lung of tremor green

and eyes of all expressions, be it
somber, wise, or warning, they teach

us the suffering of growth, of wounds
by which we reach toward the sun,
our origins owed to forest fires.

The Collage Artist
(for mom)

She knows that falling stars are not so rare,
after all. Back then, she was not looking up.
Back then, she was not falling asleep

in the right places. Now she awakes before
the birds, and sees the stars extinguish
one by one, crossing behind the mid-flight

velvet patches of hurried bats. Her heart is tied
to a silvery home, somewhere way up there,
a northern ice-bound rock, fading into the silent

blackened bark of night. Bring her the stars.
Bring her the heads which need remaking,
bring her the discarded roadside. And the wings

of finches, and the garden's broken, buried glass.
She is a builder of worlds, worker of the god-
smeared pages. Hold out your hands, full of life's
sorrowful detritus. She will know what to do.

The Walking Rock

Walk until, unheeded, mile after
mile, the neurons cease their firing.

Walk until you find new sides of hunger. Until
the copper of your exhalations is a joy.

Walk into unity, into wrecklessness, to infection.
Walk into a new skin, pull out your hair by the knot,

walk up, and down, backtrack, snag your arms on
acacia thorn. Walk faceless, swim, and grow hair, let it

dry in the sun, wet the soil w/ your animal body,
learn your scent, listen to the bees, and bash your hands

on rocks. Go wild, go mad. Walk until you transcend,
walk to shorten the list of needs, walk yawe, walk to the shores

of loneliness, sink, and become a fish in the beak of a bird.
Transform, become shit, you dying carbon idiot.

Walk and see the burnt sprout new growth.
Be covered always in the salt of your insides.

Walk until you must stay in motion to live.
Walk until the sun echoes in your flesh

in the evenings; warm patchwork of fever
that lets you know you're healing,

beneath the bone. Spirals of chill,
blister and peel to a new skin. Walk until

you lick the bowl clean. Walk your hips
into arguments w/ their sockets, walk until

your knees take turns holding pain. Walk thru
the twinges that threaten to stay with you,

walk until something vital snaps.
Walk until a song forms, walk until you're humming

w/ no one else around. Walk until you hold things
in your teeth, until you could chew

barbed wire to get free. Walk from water, to water, to
water, then move on. Walk.

Walk further than you ever have.
Walk until you can see mountains

in every direction. Until your nails blacken
and give way to crowding blister. Walk until

you are overgrown, and walk most of the way alone.
Walk dirt into your ankles. Walk red, and unsteady,

walk in wind, well before
you're ready. Walk to summits, and saddles

and creek beds. Walk the wars out
of your head.

www.ingramcontent.com/pod-product-compliance
Lightning Source LLC
Chambersburg PA
CBHW022123090426
42743CB00008B/979